The *Thing* in the Closet

Contents

Chris Powling
Illustrated by Jon Stuart

Steck Vaughn®

HOUGHTON MIFFLIN HARCOURT
Supplemental Publishers

www.SteckVaughn.com
800-531-5015

Chapter 1 – Lost and Found

Jet was in a bad mood.

"I didn't kick the ball," he grumbled. "I just dropped it."

"Three times?" laughed Kat. "No wonder Miss Jones took the ball away from you."

"I am captain of the soccer team. That means I've got to practice."

"Well, you'll have to practice being nice to Miss Jones if you want your ball back," said Max.

3

Jet watched Miss Jones open the door to the storage closet and put the ball inside. She pushed the door shut.

Chapter 2 – Spiders

Miss Jones lifted a finger to her lips. "Listen up!" she said. "For today's drama lesson, I want you all to be spiders."

Jet sat very still. His face was as white as the lines on a soccer field. He was very scared of spiders.

Miss Jones crept round the hall like a spider. "I want you all to spin an invisible web across every part of this hall."

"Invisible web!" snorted Jet. He decided to make *himself* invisible instead.

Jet crept to the back of the hall.
He turned the dial on his watch and . . .

"Where's Jet?" whispered Max a few moments later.

"I think I can guess," Kat sighed. "Look!"
She pointed at her watch. A small red dot was flashing on it. It meant that Jet had shrunk. The dot moved around the watch.

"Oh, no!" said Max.

Chapter 3 – The Thing

The storage closet was dark and gloomy. Jet tapped the flashlight button on his watch and looked around.

Jet's ball was in the lost and found box.
He grinned and climbed up to get it. Jet
pulled himself up onto the edge of the box.

Suddenly his watch started flashing.

"X-bot alert?" said Jet, reading the words on the screen. "What does that mean?"

He heard a noise behind him. It sounded like the patter of tiny feet . . . tiny, spidery feet. Slowly, Jet turned around. That's when he saw the Thing.

AHH!
Bleep!
X1
N.A.S.T.I.

Meanwhile . . .

"Good job, everybody!" called Miss Jones. "I've never seen such great spiders or such an amazing web! Now, stay as still as you can. Remember, we're trying to catch a fly!"

"I'd rather catch Jet," Max muttered.

"He's in the closet," whispered Kat.

"Come on," said Max. "Let's get him out before Miss Jones sees that he's gone!"

They crept slowly toward the closet.

Chapter 4 – In the Closet

The Thing bleeped and stepped forward. Jet screamed and stepped back. The lost and found box began to rock like a seesaw. The Thing came towards Jet.

"Help! Help!" he shouted. "It's a, a . . ."

Jet did not know what it was, but it looked very spidery.

Jet jumped off the box. He grabbed one of the jump ropes and swung across the closet. The box fell from the shelf and flipped the Thing high in the air.

The box and the Thing landed on a net full of soccerballs. The net burst open. The balls bounced around wildly.

"I don't need this much soccer practice!" Jet howled.

Luckily, he spotted his own ball coming toward him. Quickly, he dived like a goalie through one of the holes and hid inside.

N.A.S.T.i.

The Thing tumbled past Jet. It was bleeping. It looked just as scared as he was. Jet stared at it in surprise.

Chapter 5 – Good Drama

The drama class had never been so quiet. Everyone was looking at the storage closet.

"That didn't sound like a fly, Miss Jones," someone gasped. "It sounded like a herd of elephants!"

"It sounded like Jet to me!" said Max quietly.

Miss Jones walked over to the storage closet and threw open the door. This was a big mistake. There was a clattering and tumbling as everything spilled out onto the floor.

"Don't worry, Miss Jones!" said Max, quick as a flash. "Kat and I will help you clean it up."

Nobody noticed as Kat picked up Jet inside his plastic ball. She hurried out of the way to the other side of the hall. Jet crawled out of the ball. A moment later, he was big again.

As they were cleaning up, Miss Jones stepped on something. "Oh, dear," she cried out. "I think I've broken one of the toys in the lost and found box." She held it out.

It was the Thing. It looked all squashed. It was not bleeping anymore.

"Miss Jones," said Max. "Can I try and fix it? I'll get my friend Leo to help."

"Thank you, Max," said Miss Jones, as she handed him the squashed Thing. Then she looked around.

"Look at Jet, everyone!" she exclaimed. "He's still hunched-up like a spider. Now that's what I call good drama!"

Find out more . . .

Want to find out what happens to the Thing? Then read *Message in an X-Bot*.